I Can Be Anything!

I CAN BE A WRITER

By Michou Franco

Please visit our website, www.garethstevens.com. For a free color catalog of all our high-quality books, call toll free 1-800-542-2595 or fax 1-877-542-2596.

Cataloging-in-Publication Data

Names: Franco, Michou.
Title: I can be a writer / Michou Franco.
Description: New York : Gareth Stevens Publishing, 2018. | Series: I can be anything! | Includes index.
Identifiers: ISBN 9781482463378 (pbk.) | ISBN 9781482463392 (library bound) | ISBN 9781482463385 (6 pack)
Subjects: LCSH: Authorship–Vocational guidance–Juvenile literature. | Writing services–Vocational guidance–Juvenile literature.
Classification: LCC PN159.F73 2018 | DDC 808.02–dc23

First Edition

Published in 2018 by
Gareth Stevens Publishing
111 East 14th Street, Suite 349
New York, NY 10003

Copyright © 2018 Gareth Stevens Publishing

Editor: Therese Shea
Designer: Sarah Liddell

Photo credits: Cover, pp. 1, 13, 17 (kid) Early Spring/Shutterstock.com; cover, p. 1 (background) ImageFlow/Shutterstock.com; pp. 5, 7 Rawpixel.com/Shutterstock.com; pp. 9, 21, 24 (wood background) BravissimoS/Shutterstock.com; pp. 9, 24 (newspaper) goir/Shutterstock.com; p. 11 JohnKwan/Shutterstock.com; pp. 13, 17 (background) Africa Studio/Shutterstock.com; p. 15 Yuganov Konstantin/Shutterstock.com; pp. 19, 24 (library) AN NGUYEN/Shutterstock.com; p. 21 (book) Joanna Dorota/Shutterstock.com; p. 23 Syda Productions/Shutterstock.com.

All rights reserved. No part of this book may be reproduced in any form without permission in writing from the publisher, except by a reviewer.

Printed in the United States of America

CPSIA compliance information: Batch #CS17GS: For further information contact Gareth Stevens, New York, New York at 1-800-542-2595.

Contents

My mom is a writer.

Mom writes
for a newspaper.
She writes
about our city.

Mom writes stories
that are true.
True stories are nonfiction.

NEWS

WORLD

BUSINESS

SCIENCE

SPORTS

Some people write stories that aren't true. These stories are fiction.

Once upon a time . . .

I want to write, too!
What will I write?

I could write a play.
My friends could act!

I will write
a children's book.
I like those books best.

First, I read books
at the library.
Then, I write a story.
Last, I draw pictures.

Here's my book!

Fluffy Goes
on a Walk

I can be a writer.
So can you!

Words to Know

library

newspaper

Index